Hot Potato
mealtime rhymes

Selected by Neil Philip
Illustrated by Claire Henley

CLARION BOOKS
New York

For Madeleine Rose
—C.H.

For Daniel and Beatrice Dendy
—N.P.

The Old Man of the Coast

There was an old man of the coast,
Who placidly sat on a post;
   But when it was cold
   He relinquished his hold
And called for some hot buttered toast.

Edward Lear

My Mouth

stays shut
    but
food just
finds
    a way

        my tongue says
we are
    full today
    but
        teeth just
            grin
    and
    say
        come in
i am always hungry

Arnold Adoff

Me, Myself, and I

Me, myself, and I—
We went to the kitchen and ate a pie.
Then my mother, she came in
And chased us out with a rolling pin.

Anonymous

Mommy Slept Late and Daddy Fixed Breakfast

Daddy fixed the breakfast.
He made us each a waffle.
It looked like gravel pudding.
It tasted something awful.

"Ha, ha," he said, "I'll try again.
This time I'll get it right."
But what *I* got was in between
Bituminous and anthracite.

"A little too well done? Oh well,
I'll have to start all over."
That time what landed on my plate
Looked like a manhole cover.

I tried to cut it with a fork:
The fork gave off a spark.
I tried a knife and twisted it
Into a question mark.

I tried it with a hack-saw.
I tried it with a torch.
It didn't even make a dent.
It didn't even scorch.

The next time Dad gets breakfast
When Mommy's sleeping late,
I think I'll skip the waffles.
I'd sooner eat the plate!

John Ciardi

Yellow Butter

Yellow butter purple jelly red jam black bread

Spread it thick
Say it quick

Yellow butter purple jelly red jam black bread

Spread it thicker
Say it quicker

Yellow butter purple jelly red jam black bread

Now repeat it
While you eat it

Yellow butter purple jelly red jam black bread

Don't talk
With your mouth full!

Mary Ann Hoberman

Cake Mistake

Mother made a birthday cake,
For icing she used glue.
The children sit so quiet now,
Andchewandchewandchew.

Douglas Florian

Mix a Pancake

Mix a pancake,
Stir a pancake,
    Pop it in the pan;
Fry the pancake,
Toss the pancake—
    Catch it if you can.

Christina Rossetti

Oh My Goodness, Oh My Dear

Oh my goodness, oh my dear,
Sassafras & ginger beer,
Chocolate cake & apple punch:
I'm too full to eat my lunch.

Clyde Watson

Hot Food

We sit down to eat
and the potato's a bit hot
so I only put a little bit on my fork
and I blow
whooph whooph
until it's cool
just cool
then into the mouth
nice.
And there's my brother
he's doing the same
whooph whooph
into the mouth
nice.
There's my mum
she's doing the same
whooph whooph
into the mouth
nice.

But my dad.
My dad.
What does he do?
He stuffs a great big chunk of potato
into his mouth.
Then
that really does it.
His eyes pop out
he flaps his hands
he blows, he puffs, he yells
he bobs his head up and down
he spits bits of potato
all over his plate
and he turns to us and says,
"Watch out everybody—
the potato's very hot."

Michael Rosen

The Spoon

Before I eat my pudding,
   I often stop to see
If someone in my pudding-spoon
   Is really, really me;
For up and down they are so thin
   And sideways they're so fat,
I don't believe it's possible
   That I can look like that!

Elizabeth Fleming

You Must Never Bath in an Irish Stew

You must never bath in an Irish Stew
It's a most illogical thing to do
   But should you persist against my reasoning
   Don't fail to add the appropriate seasoning.

Spike Milligan

Beautiful Soup

Beautiful Soup, so rich and green,
Waiting in a hot tureen!
Who for such dainties would not stoop?
Soup of the evening, beautiful Soup!
Soup of the evening, beautiful Soup!

   Beau–ootiful Soo–oop!
   Beau–ootiful Soo–oop!
Soo–oop of the e–e–evening,
   Beautiful, beautiful Soup!

Beautiful Soup! Who cares for fish,
Game, or any other dish?
Who would not give all else for two p
ennyworth only of beautiful Soup?
Pennyworth only of beautiful Soup?

   Beau–ootiful Soo–oop!
   Beau–ootiful Soo–oop!
Soo–oop of the e–e–evening,
   Beautiful, beauti–FUL SOUP!

Lewis Carroll

SOUP

Baby's Drinking Song

Sip a little
Sup a little
     From your little
Cup a little
     Sup a little
Sip a little
     Put it to your
Lip a little
     Tip a little
Tap a little
     Not into your
Lap or it'll
     Drip a little
Drop a little
     On the table
Top a little.

James Kirkup

Rice Pudding

What is the matter with Mary Jane?
She's crying with all her might and main,
And she won't eat her dinner—rice pudding again—
What *is* the matter with Mary Jane?

What is the matter with Mary Jane?
I've promised her dolls and a daisy-chain,
And a book about animals—all in vain—
What *is* the matter with Mary Jane?

What is the matter with Mary Jane?
She's perfectly well, and she hasn't a pain;
But, look at her, now she's beginning again!—
What *is* the matter with Mary Jane?

What is the matter with Mary J
I've promised her sweets and a
And I've begged her to stop fo
What *is* the matter with Mar

What is the matter with Mary J
She's perfectly well and she has
And it's lovely rice pudding for dinn
What *is* the matter with Mary J

A.A.

Send My Spinach

Send my spinach
Off to Spain.
Parcel post it

rian

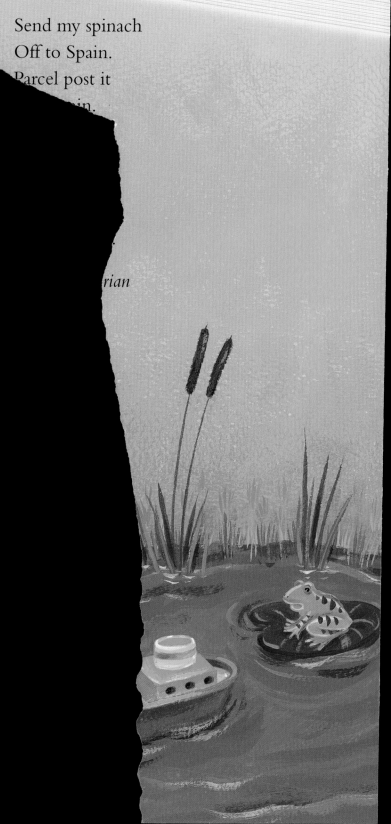

The Friendly
Cinnamon Bun

Shining in his stickiness and glistening with honey,
Safe among his sisters and his brothers on a tray,
With raisin eyes that looked at me as I put down my money,
There smiled a friendly cinnamon bun, and this I heard him say:

"It's a lovely, lovely morning, and the world's a lovely place;
I know it's going to be a lovely day.
I know we're going to be good friends; I like your honest face;
Together we might go a long, long way."

The baker's girl rang up the sale, "I'll wrap your bun," said she.
"Oh no, you needn't bother," I replied.
I smiled back at that cinnamon bun and ate him, one two three,
And walked out with his friendliness inside.

Russell Hoban

If I Were
King of Sweden

If I were King of Sweden
I would never wear a crown,
But I'd ride in a golden carriage
With the window down.

I would wake up very early
In my palace by the sea;
I would breakfast on marshmallow
And have the same for tea.

Each day would be my birthday,
I'd buy fizzy drink in kegs;
Once a month there'd be an Easter
With enormous Easter eggs.

If I saw a man or woman
Who looked hungry in the street,
I'd invite them in for dinner
And give them pies to eat.

If I were King of Sweden
I'd go walking to and fro,
And every person that I met
Would stop and say, "Hullo!"

James K. Baxter

Three Little Ghostesses

Three little ghostesses,
Sitting on postesses,
Eating buttered toastesses,
Greasing their fistesses,
Up to the wristesses,
Oh, what beastesses
To make such feastesses!

Anonymous

ACKNOWLEDGMENTS

We thank the following copyright holders for permission to reprint individual poems, as listed below. Every effort has been made to trace copyright holders, and we will be pleased to correct any errors or omissions in future editions.

HarperCollins Publishers for "My Mouth" by Arnold Adoff from *Eats* (Lothrop, Lee & Shepard, 1979), copyright © 1979 by Arnold Adoff; The James Baxter Foundation for "If I Were King of Sweden" by James K. Baxter, first published in *Collected Poems* by James K. Baxter (Oxford University Press, Australia & New Zealand, 1988); HarperCollins Publishers for "Mommy Slept Late and Daddy Fixed Breakfast" by John Ciardi, from *You Read to Me, I'll Read to You* (Lippincott, 1962), copyright © 1962 by John Ciardi; "The Spoon" by Elizabeth Fleming is taken from *Gammon and Spinach* (W. Collins, 1927), copyright 1927 by Elizabeth Fleming; "Cake Mistake" and "Send My Spinach" from *Bing Bang Boing*, copyright © 1994 by Douglas Florian, reprinted by permission of Harcourt, Inc.; David Higham Associates for "The Friendly Cinnamon Bun" by Russell Hoban, from *The Pedaling Man* (Heinemann), copyright © 1968 by Russell Hoban; "Yellow Butter," copyright © 1981 by Mary Ann Hoberman, from *The Llama Who Had No Pajama: 100 Favorite Poems* by Mary Ann Hoberman, reprinted by permission of Harcourt, Inc.; "Baby's Drinking Song" by James Kirkup, from *White Shadow, Black Shadow* (Dent, 1970), reprinted by permission of the author; Spike Milligan Productions Limited for "You Must Never Bath in an Irish Stew" by Spike Milligan, from *Silly Verse for Kids* (Puffin, 1968); "Rice Pudding" by A. A. Milne, from *When We Were Very Young* by A. A. Milne, illustrations by E. H. Shepard, copyright 1924 by E. P. Dutton, renewed 1952 by A. A. Milne. Used by permission of Dutton Children's Books, a division of Penguin Young Readers Group, a member of Penguin Group (USA) Inc., 345 Hudson St., New York, NY 10014. All rights reserved; PFD for "Hot Food" by Michael Rosen, from *The Hypnotiser and Other Skyfoogling Poems* (André Deutsch, 1988), copyright © 1988 by Michael Rosen; HarperCollins Publishers for "Oh My Goodness, Oh My Dear" by Clyde Watson from *Father Fox's Pennyrhymes* (Thomas Y. Crowell, 1971), copyright © 1971 by Clyde Watson.

Clarion Books
a Houghton Mifflin Company imprint
215 Park Avenue South, New York, NY 10003

Published in the United States in 2004 by arrangement with
The Albion Press Ltd., Spring Hill, Idbury, Oxfordshire OX7 6RU, England

Compilation copyright © 2004 by Neil Philip
Illustrations copyright © 2004 by Claire Henley
For copyright of individual poems, see the acknowledgments above.

Designed by Emma Bradford

The illustrations were executed in acrylic paint on paper.
The text was set in 15-point Bembo.
The headings were hand-lettered by Alan Peacock.

For information about permission to reproduce selections from this book, write to
Permissions, Houghton Mifflin Company, 215 Park Avenue South, New York, NY 10003.

www.houghtonmifflinbooks.com

ISBN: 0-618-31554-3

Full cataloging information is available from the Library of Congress.

10 9 8 7 6 5 4 3 2 1

Typesetting: Servis Filmsetting Ltd, Manchester
Color origination: Classicscan, Singapore
Printed in Hong Kong/China by South China Printing Co.